C000053057

A UNITY OF VOICES

Edited by

Becki Mee

LOOK INSIDE

Was skin tone man's invention?
To show the difference his intention?
Or was our God to blame,
For not making us all look the same?
Why must the press make aggravation,
By drawing attention to race relation?
Every story that they write,
Tells if someone is black or white.
They just push people far apart,
It's what is inside someone's heart.
What of colour do we care?
Why is the reference always there?
If you're said to pay your rates,
Tell your skin tone it always states.
Do they want to start a war?
What is the colour reference for?
Can't we all just pretend,
We don't see the colour of our faces.
Sit and have a welcome drink,
About our neighbours kindly think.
If we look far and wide,
It's the man who is inside.

Colin Allsop

MOTHER

Drifting stellar dust and gasses,
Big bang, sun, planets and the earth.
One of the most enduring mysteries.
Our beautiful planet had its birth.

And then there was man.
And woman. And creation.
Blues and greens and all the hues.
Colours of this beautiful nation.

What a lovely eco system.
Colours and species, so many to see,
Seas, mountains, flowers of all kinds,
Butterfly, dragonfly, and the bee.

So what happened, thousands of years later.
The Result, have baited breath.

And does the world care at all?
As she sheds her tears of blood.
Mankind has raped Mother Earth.
I am empty. Greed is the God.

Brian Haswell

UP, UP AND AWAY!

Went up on the roller coaster - while Mum remained below,
Brave of me to go alone. That I've now found out and know,
But it was foolish too - as more frightening than first thought.
Food went on an upward rush - as the thrill I sought
Went up and down at speed. Recklessly it seemed,
Seemed also at times to outer space - like Scottie I was beamed,
As I whipped round the corners, most of me was numb,
At the utmost climax, my stomach remained at top,
                    while contents rained on my mum!

John L Wright & 'Jackdaw'

BOYS

Boys, boys, boys
God I don't know why?
Boys are everywhere, here and there,
Side by side, back or front of you.

Boys can be cheeky, boys can be noisy
They get up to everything, instead of being good.
I think this last verse, will describe them perfectly.

Calling you names, it wouldn't be like them
Fighting with you, has to describe them
Talking and making fun of you, they love a lot
Noisy is definitely the word for them.

Sarah Louise Magee (13)

MODIFIED WORLD

Nutants ugly creeping ivy weeds
Covered forests pastures Frankinstein seeds
Forever gone lush evergreen fields
Tormentedly mother nature she reels
Scientists genetically misguided nature messed
Carried out unnatural biological test
Strange pollen shrouded pastures deadly green
Mile upon mile quiet silent scene
Gone pretty countryside shrubs
Eternity blasted forever troublesome slugs
Insects species completely obliterated
Nature serene wonders so violated
Man destroyed planet perfectly formed
Wouldn't listen yet they were warned

Ann Hathaway

THOSE RAINFORESTS

Those rainforests get less and less
So the world is put to the test
For as we cut down more and more
Soon there will be none left in store.

Those rainforests get less and less
And all the land is ploughed up
For food for us yet it is good enough
For they spray on it this and that
Until there are no bugs left to put in your hat.

Those rainforests get less and less
Until now there is none
Even we as people do not have long
But who really can we blame
Just everybody who thought the same.

Keith L Powell

THE BEES' LAST SONG, AS MAN DESTROYS
THE BALANCE OF NATURE

I made you wax
I made you honey.
You ate my honey,
You took my wax.
You took my wax
And made a candle.
You took the candle
Down into your mine.
One day, the flame went out:
That day you left the mine.
You brought the candle up,
Up into the air,
And the flame went out.
The flame went out
And the world went dark.
The world went dark
And I was no more: no more
To make you honey;
No more
To make you wax.

Alan Brinsley

THE END OF THE WORLD

Shock and horror!
Can you believe it?
The world is ending tomorrow!
Only the devil could cause such a dilemma.

Some say they have been preparing for this for years,
while others say how could it be?
And end up in tears,
the devil laughs and says who cares.

Billions of people will be killed
and you can bet the devil is thrilled.
For when Armageddon comes,
God will fit the bill.

The four horsemen of the apocalypse will rise up.
War and death will cause there to be no more.
Famine and pestilence will make it the final score.
As in *The revelation of St John the divine.*

War on a black steed, death on a white steed,
famine on a pale steed and pestilence on a red steed.
They will ride above the seven seas,
destroy at the devil's please.

Where are all the heroes?
For this is a poor show, indeed.
Trapped on this evil world with nowhere to go.
'Never give up' says brave aunty Jo.

God ponders the way it goes,
should he disperse the thunder and greyness of clouds,
or rebuild the cracked earth
and put right the devil's curse.

He releases his fearsome celestial armies
so evil will pay for its crimes,
against his beloved humanity
and as always good triumphs over the devil's insanity.

Ali Sebastian

ON WAKING TO A SNOWY MORNING

Twirling and twirling, the snowflakes are falling.
Who has ever seen anything half as beautiful?
But in the morning all this shining world
Will have disappeared.
Only the snowman will remain
And with the coming of the morning sun
He too will slowly, tearfully, fade away.

Lee Chadwick

THE DOT

I am a dot, just not any dot
Nor am I a forward slash or a backward slash
No, no, I am a superior dot
I am a BBC Co-Dot.

David G Bromage

HOME FROM HOME

'Come live with me and be my love.'
The rumbling tones of mighty Mars
made welcome ever warring man.
'Pray, sup full of horrors at my feast,
you will enjoy the plates of flesh and blood.
You'll revel in the vistas that lead straight to hell.'
The stealthy terrorist is my delight,
hooked on the bullet's whine, the hidden bomb.
Now, let us finish off this festive meal
with anguished tears which make a toxic brew,
but if you have no stomach for the fight
I'll show you subtle ways
which will extend your killing fields;
Finance your famines
nurture the seeds of pestilence.
Chaos - rediscovered is my battle ground;
Huge asteroids I hurl from outer space
when weaklings dare to challenge me
as earnestly they strive for puny peace
but - here's the rub -
they must stand up and make a fight for it!
My Martian laughter rocks the universe
as still we kill - they kill - all kill.
Traveller, you may come to Mars and rest in peace.

A L Baldwin

SPORTING ACTIVITIES

With ten buttery thumbs
and two left feet
I was never really destined
to be an athlete

our PE teacher would tactfully
put me in goal defence
where I basically
just jumped up and down

waving my arms around
like you do, when you're five foot two
trying in vain to distract
a six foot giant in plimsolls

truth is I was hopeless
at netball and sporting activities
and had only ever come first
once, in an egg and spoon race
sponsored by Wrigleys.

Heather Kirkpatrick

THE PORTER

A general porter I was once
At a hospital called St James,
A fine head porter was in charge
With whom we did not play games.

At seven the morning work was begun
So we had to wake up very early,
The job was to move trolleys around
So physically one had to be burly.

Arthur, Thomas, Joseph were my friends
And we made a wonderful crowd,
'Though our work was ordinary
Our spirits remained unbowed.

It was said, and it's very true,
That a hospital's run by nurses,
But without porters it cannot do
With adequate money in their purses.

Casualty, X-ray, physiotherapy,
The porters departments are many,
Moving patients to and fro
Was work to make one happy.

W Fred Tabaczynski

CHANGE IN VIEWS

On the playground in primary school,
boys were thought of as very uncool.
With their dirty, smelly, torn clothes,
and their constantly running smudged noses.

In secondary school things do seem to alter
and those rough stinking boys become cuter.
Their eyes start to shine and they smile so nice,
girls become their girlfriends in just a trice.

By college time girls and boys are together,
some get engaged, so this is forever.
But throughout the changing ageing years,
boys cause girls a lot of tears.

Kay Davies

First published in Great Britain in 1999 by
POETRY NOW
Remus House,
Coltsfoot Drive,
Woodston,
Peterborough, PE2 9JX
Telephone (01733) 898101
Fax (01733) 313524

All Rights Reserved

Copyright Contributors 1999

HB ISBN 0 75430 743 3
SB ISBN 0 75430 744 1

FOREWORD

Although we are a nation of poets we are accused of not reading poetry, or buying poetry books. After many years of listening to the incessant gripes of poetry publishers, I can only assume that the books they publish, in general, are books that most people do not want to read.

Poetry should not be obscure, introverted, and as cryptic as a crossword puzzle: it is the poet's duty to reach out and embrace the world.

The world owes the poet nothing and we should not be expected to dig and delve into a rambling discourse searching for some inner meaning.

The reason we write poetry (and almost all of us do) is because we want to communicate: an ideal; an idea; or a specific feeling. Poetry is as essential in communication, as a letter; a radio; a telephone, and the main criteria for selecting the poems in this anthology is very simple: they communicate.

CONTENTS

ECLIPSE 1999

First touch moon's face
past our sun
darkening hand placed
over the sky

Shadows snuffed out
fast spreading
darkness brings wind
guidless memory

Time's slow shadow
pulls back
hand opens/fingers spread
light returns

T Webster

POEM

My sister wants my poems to rhyme,
To write blank verse is just a crime,
'It isn't poetry if it doesn't rhyme,'
She says, and really must keep time,
By scanning line by line.

Yet it would be as much a crime,
To make it rhyme, yes, every time,
And truth to say I see no point in trying.

As apple blossom scents the springtime day,
With sultry summer on the way,
I have a more melodious tune to play.

The lambs have gambolled, swallow's here,
Those bees are buzzing, never fear,
That sun is shining, sky is clear.

Let's walk the forest, breathe the air,
Then snuggle down in that comfy chair.

Paul Butters

CONTEMPLATION

Lost in meditation
By a silver spring,
Thinking all the
Many thoughts
That solitude can bring.
Dreaming of the future,
Dwelling on the past –
All the gains and losses,
And the love
That failed to last.
And so life's path continues,
Forever up and down –
One moment you're a hero,
The next you are a clown.
And if, like me,
You're stranded
Very high and dry,
Remember there's tomorrow,
And the sun's
Still in the sky.

V B D'Wit

BUTTERFLIES IN AMBER

Memories come and settle in the mind
And set like butterflies in amber. They
Come with the seemingly mundane, without
Warning. They are the surprise components –

Of ordinary things. A child's dress all but
Finished, the sight of curtains drawn against
The summer heat, furniture gleaming with
Lavender wax or a flowerbed fenced –

In against intruders. Shadows of leaves
On water, unkempt daisy-speckled lawns,
Wallflowers all bright and grown dense, heady
With perfume, butterflies resting in swarms –

Resting like recalled memories settling
Forever like butterflies in amber.

Margaret Hibbert

FLOW OF TEARS

A gushing roar of water falls
deafeningly
plunges
over rapids
churns
through pebbles
consumes
silent screams

frothy turbulence swells
engulfs
murky debris
pounds
unsettled rocks
embraces
unshed streams
of overwhelming tears

the river washes
the river cleanses
the river carries
all loss
all grief
all sadness
gently, water flows softly onwards
calmer, deeper, clearer, stronger.

Katrina Shepherd

GOSSAMER DREAM

We dream our dream and always will
of intertwining fingers' touch
on rivers winding shaded tree-banked
forest green and love that's such
an understanding deep-grooved tree-bark
thread of thoughts and deepest knowing
like the veins on gentle wings
of dragonflies and fireflies glowing
so this our pleasant mystery hush
see diamond stars in soft dark sky
we dream as one in meadows moon-bathed
ours is not to reason why.

This our sharing such uniqueness
fingerprints like tree-bark lines
with no beginning no known ending
far beyond the realms of time
and always known needs no explaining
mirrored feelings thoughts and themes
live today and wish tomorrow
sweeter threads of gossamer dreams.

David Taub

WHAT EYE COULD READ?

Under Lunar's lustrous light I lie
And contemplate the Astral sky.
Is just one star meant for me,
Or do constellations say what's to be?

Each life fills its time and space.
What more can enter this personal place?
Nothing's still: I go my way,
Earth, moon, sun, stars go where they may.
What relationship there of mine,
Could any mortal man divine?

You think that each day a page must turn?
Look close, look closer: you'll discern
Not lines, not words, but single letters change.
Each minute, each second, some rearrange.
What eye could read from such a book
A single second in a lifelong look?

R L Cooper

MY ANGEL

A Guardian Angel she became at six,
Without a say in when or why,
Not knowing how long for, as passing time it ticks,
Never to complain, nor to utter a sigh.

A role of motherhood and caring,
She took on the task without complaining,
Having to cope with all others staring,
As each step her mother struggled with gaining.

At the age of six she matured with haste,
To reach a helping hand to her crippled mother,
Of childhood and laughter she'd only had a taste,
Though she never wished for her life to be another.

Eighteen long months now passed through, she's seven and a half,
So strong and kind, her love consumes all those around,
Now her mother slowly mends she has time to laugh,
A child with care and compassion for that in life which she has found.

So beautiful and kind, a blossoming flower,
With my heart I wish her dearly all the best,
A future so full of luck, created from her inner strength and power,
Although it is not to be planned but only to be guessed.

Rebecca Simmonds

MEMORIES OF LITTLE CHRISTMAS

The festive season almost over
and the excitement of seeing new
faces visit our small farm over
for another year as relations
and neighbours calling for
Christmas ceases. Lonesome for
the red berried holly and the crib
packed away with the brass candlesticks.
Missing the cosy atmosphere of bright
crepe decorations, cards and posters
with Merry Christmas, Happy New Year
placed in old shoeboxes. Letters
that came with parcels from America
left aside for answering. Having to
wait twelve months for Christmas cake,
plum pudding and the extra groceries
from Murray's shop in the town, and
the local Co-op; time seems infinite.

Mary Guckian

AN IRREVERENT WEAVE

I wonder if I maybe could
Make my words fit this Taubin form;
My brain really has understood,
Take rhyming ends as the new norm.

But I must not show such faint heart
For Ian suggests we show panache,
Cut the cackle and down to art,
Cor – to call this such, is just rash!

Blow your trumpet IW said,
There, I'll continue with this rhyme,
Crow loud and long, not fear to tread
Where angels trod another time.

Now it's over bar the shouting,
Who will be the lucky winner?
Bow out Marj dear, there's no doubting
You are too much of a sinner.

M Haddon

DAWN CHORUS

I love to hear you
Singing the morning's praises,
Beautiful dawn-birds
Waking me at the sunrise,
Starting my day with love songs.

Mary Hunt

THE MOMENT – FIRST

Alas! The precious moment passed by
The moment when our eyes and souls met.
In the bustling crowd, we came together
The pushing, then the unexpectedness
That startling surprise meeting face to face
Left me wondrous, breathless and speechless
The searching look deep down in our eyes
Was answered by our hearts, we both knew . . .
A shy half smile followed and then nothing
If only I had managed to speak out
If only you had spoken to me.
But you were gone, out of my life forever
Gone with a longing look and a tear
Taking with you, my broken heart.

T Daley

MY TIME

Footsteps in the sand,
They belong to me
I walk across the sand,
And head towards the sea.

I walk along its edge
With the breeze upon my face,
Time has stopped still,
No worries, no strife.

Just me and the sea
And the sand and the breeze,
No one to please, but myself.

L Tweedy

DEWDROPS

The mirror image of my soul
Held in the drops of dew
With crystal clear transparency
Reflects a sky so blue

I rest a while on leaves so green
And hills of a different hue
I settle in the heart of a rose
So safe in thoughts of you

But as I touch and taste and feel
And learn just how to be
I embrace the heart that gave me
The ears and eyes to see.

Helen Arnold

THE BALLAD OF STEPHEN HAWKINGS

If
Professor Hawkings
Be a Tarot symbol
Which is he to be?
A minor secret
The Scum of the Universe
Or a trump player
Whistling out stardust
In the cosmic landscape
Would he swap his
Wheelchair for an
Upturned cross
Swinging between
Heaven and Earth
Letting his mind
Soar free in
Einstein's universe
Getting hung up
On the speed of light
For a view beyond birth
A Vision Questor
Seeking the faces of Janus
In the
Atoms of Conception

Stephen Goggin

LYTHAM ROAD

I walked out of John's
On to Lytham Road,
Summer hung in the air
Like the smell of candlewax
In a small room.
I thought of the two
Repeats I'd just watched

On his Sky.
I was only six when they
Were on first.
I remembered sitting round
The fire, waiting for
Someone to make the tea,
And wondering who was

Going out for the next
Bucket of coal.
The smell of my father's pipe
Stinking the room,
And a tawny picture of Jesus
Hanging above the mantelpiece.
Small screen magnetism,

Divine imperialism.
Now the place lies dead
Like the leaves on his grave,
I caught those years on
Lytham Road
Black promises and broken dreams,
Time lost.

Paul O'Neill

TOGETHER . . .

(Written in memory of the sudden loss of a beloved friend)

Together. Taken
Suddenly without warning.
Parted. Time stood still.
Not true, not real, cannot be.
Dreams lost, abandoned, tears flow.

Ann

WHAT MAKES A POEM?

I'm wrestling with a knotty problem
One which I can't quite define.
When is a poem not a poem?
Is it when it doesn't rhyme?

Or when there is no rhythmic meter,
Doesn't really seem to flow,
Can free verse be called poetic?
I must confess I do not know.

Three samples were discussed at length
At our creative writing bee.
The first, free verse, split up the class
With 'Was it prose or poetry?'

The second, though it didn't rhyme,
Flowed very easy on the ear,
Borne along right to the end
The rhythmic beat was very clear.

The third was rhymed by Betjamin,
Exposing evils of our day.
Crumbling marriage, loveless lives,
Mad road-rage taking lives away.

So I've come to the conclusion,
No matter what form poems take,
The appeal is in the rhythm
And the music words can make.

If it grabs instant attention
From the first or second line,
If it makes your pulse beat faster
Or you savour it like wine.

If it plays on your emotions
With a maestro's practised hand,
Puts you there among the action
In Imagination Land.

When the final line is ended,
Then you really must agree,
If your heart and mind were made to sing,
Then it's surely poetry.

F Gerrard

LONDON, 1944

A bombed-out backstreet. Up against a wall.
His army greatcoat wrapped around them both.
Her practised hands hoist up her Wren-blue skirt.
A moment's passion while the whole world burns.

Her husband is at sea; his wife's at home,
Flirting with GIs from a South Coast base.
Marriage vows crumble under heavy fire
From new-found freedom and 'Live for today'.

Phil Webster

THE WINDOW OF LIFE

She had never understood
Why all this had happened, yet –
She was the outsider.
Understanding never portrayed,
She was never acknowledged.
The door was shut in her face.
All were oblivious,
To her inner feelings.
All blame placed on her shoulders.
She was isolated,
Unwanted, unworthy, unclean, unloved.
Filled with guilt.
Constantly needing to punish herself.

The years passed by,
Age took its toll, but –
Try as she may again and again,
Never would it be any different.
Life now had the feeling of –
Rain streaming down the windows
On a warm summer day.
Everything had been spoilt,
All faith in others destroyed,
Trust in everyone washed away
With the raindrops.
Life was simply to be endured.
Never again to be enjoyed.

Jemma Jackson

ANOTHER SATURDAY NIGHT

Lying in the bath,
bottle of wine already half-empty,
I'm happy but slightly uneasy.
Down by my feet an army is massing,
the Scum Army.
I've seen it many times before
but tonight it looks bigger
and more powerful than usual.

What's happening?
It's beginning to advance up my leg.
Better pour myself another drink.
Down it quickly.
Pour another one.
Dutch courage is needed
(not to mention their Resistance fighters).

The army has nearly reached Private Parts.
Think of something rude.
Well done.
A small part of me is safe.
Time to celebrate and have another drink.
Make it quick though.
My chest is in grave danger
of being overrun.

Don't panic.
Launch the counterattack.
Splash! Splash! Splash!
Beat it back.
Keep splashing.
It's on the retreat.

I hear a cry in the background.
Something about the Turners
are coming in half-an-hour.
Obviously a deranged French woman
whose husband has just been shot.

Her voice sounds familiar.
It reminds me of someone
I knew before the war.
I'd like to help her
but I must be ever vigilant.
At any moment the Scum Army may regroup
and launch another offensive.

I drain the bottle.

Dave Bryan

THE FOOL AND THE TRUTH

As the sharpest shadows fall,
in defeat I gave my all.
My reflection beckons me,
sacrificial blood runs free.

Paralysed, my weakened prey,
begging for the blade to slay.
Torture me from dusk 'til dawn,
ceremonial ritual.

I have one more hour to live,
nothing left for me to give.
Shed no tears of woe for me,
I will live eternally.

Pure remorse breeds agony,
no one will remember me.
After all is said and done,
I am nothing,
I am one.

As I draw my final breath,
satisfied, I welcome death.
I embrace serenity.
Enter the void of destiny.

Do not shed a tear for me,
I am the voice within the breeze.
Do not wish for yesterday,
I am the dawn of every day.

I'll be there when you're alone,
in the darkest hour you've ever known.
I will be there forever on,
I'll wait until we two
are one.

J Hadland

THE EARTH MOVED

The bug bit hard, I sneezed and coughed –
lungs near collapsed, head near fell off.
A tourist tornado passed nearby –
we watched the clouds, prepared to fly!

Snow, hail, frost undermined our feet,
coats froze solid with icy sleet;
Honey (that's the dog) was really miffed
when wailing winds kennel did lift.

We chased escaping 'wheelie-bins',
endured water-cuts for our sins;
stared hopefully at blank TV screens,
left in darkness – techno has-beens!

Christmas itself was wonderful –
quiet, serene, but never dull;
so if you ask how it was for me . . .
Either way – the earth moved, babee!

Phoenix Martin

WAR OF THE WORLD

Look around you
And it's plain to see
How beautiful our world can be.

From the smallest ant
To the grisly bear
And the animals whose skins we wear.

Treat every living thing the same
For prejudice is a loser's game.

Respect the world of plants and flowers
For it may hold secret healing powers.

Love Mother Nature as your own
For she is not easily overthrown.

Years of pollution of the ground and air,
Has damaged the environment beyond repair.

What sort of world will we leave behind?
What problems may our children find?

Our world is dying yet we cannot see
A different view or possibility.

Jennifer Morgan (14)

A WORLD IN THE FUTURE

A world where no-one cries
A world where no-one lies,
This world cannot be
Never in eternity.

The reason for this being
That people find crying
And lying appealing.

A world where no-one hits
A world where no-one spits,
This world cannot be
Never in eternity.

The reason for this being
That people find hitting
And spitting appealing.

My future world
Will come in time,
But in the meanwhile
I will give you this rhyme.

Jordan Natalie Box (12)

HOPE FOR THE PLANET

The world was created with peace in mind,
now many years later, how could man be so blind?
Not even thinking about cutting down trees,
killing our neighbours and polluting the seas.
It doesn't take much to understand,
that if we're not careful it will kill the land.
So now the job's left with you and me,
to save the environment you can see.
To stop cutting trees down, and polluting the sea,
to save all the animals, and let them run free.
This world that we live in belongs to us all,
and the death of the planet, would be the death of us all.

Rebecca Gate (13)

DON'T KILL THE ANIMALS

Why do they do it?
I do not know,
Do they kill them for money,
for fame or for show?
There should be a law,
a ban, a guard,
Nobody should do it,
it's not fair, it's hard.
How would you feel if
you were a tiger?
Being bullied, being taken away,
being killed.
You'll have to pay
So think again,
Don't kill the animals,
They're like humans
They're like *you!*

Gemma Farina (9)

THE FUTURE WILL BE COOL

F is for flying machines, zipping through space,
U is for unusual beings, from another place.
T is for travelling, to a far off sun,
U is for universe, a place for holiday fun.
R is for robots, who teach us all in school,
E is for enjoyment, the future will be cool.

Adam Chilton

THE ENVIRONMENT TO KEEP

Have you heard what's going around,
Smoke and pollution bring the world down.
Out of all the planets in the universe,
Why is ours the one full of dirt?

People treat plants and animals bad,
While all it's doing is making us sad.
Don't throw litter, a can or a tin,
Where right in front of you there is a bin.

People go poaching, but what good does it do?
It just harms the animals but also me and you.
With all the people's and animals' deaths,
If we carry on like this, there will be nothing left.

Samantha Utting (13)

THE TITLE IS UP TO YOU!

My worst nightmare has come true,
Pain, suffering, loss of hope,
Family and friends torn apart.

Nato bombs Kosovo again!
Targeting the enemy bases,
The noise of buildings,
Falling with a '*bang*' to the ground.

Refugees, trying to get away,
Fleeing to the nearest countries,
Kosovilians, mainly men, being taken away,
Killed in front of their children's eyes.

People crying as they beg for help,
Asking for our nation's support,
Food, clothing, water and shelter,
All scarce during the long, cold hours.

Mother, father, sister, brother,
Holding out their hands,
As Tony Blair visits their camps,
Promising that everything will be alright.

Everyone praying,
To the Lord God above,
That he will help them,
To fight for another day.

Search deep down,
Into the chest of emotions,
And find a way to include,
In your prayers tonight,
That the bombings will come to an end,
And family and friends can be reunited again.

Sharon-Louise Jones (15)

POLLUTION

I look at the sky,
and wonder why,
we dump things in the river.

I look at the sky,
and wonder why,
pollution makes me quiver.

I look at the sky,
and wonder why,
we destroy animals' homes.

I look at the sky,
and wonder why,
we do this to make new traffic zones.

I look at the sky,
and wonder whether,
in the year 2000 will there be plants or trees?
We think polluting the world is clever,

God help us, please.

Joscelyne Canavan (8)

A WORLD FOR THE FUTURE

The future.
Are you thinking of silver suits,
And flying cars?
Trips to the moon,
And a perfect world?

Everything's just right,
A problem free world,
Beautiful landscapes,
And wonderful trees,

No disease or hunger,
Clean crisp air,
Nothing but happiness.
Everywhere?

Are you sure?
Look again.
It's a scientist's world,
Manufactured so we can look forward.
But is that where we're going?
Forward?

Disease and famine,
Deforestation,
Pollution,
Misery.
Things are not getting better.

Think about it.
Silver suits?
Flying cars?
A perfect world?

The future.
Now what does it mean to you?

Holly Davies (15)

POLLUTION

P ainfully unsightly things
O bviously things that are not looked after
L eads to illness
L itter
U ntreated
T ankers
I gnorant people causing it
O xygen
N oise.

Laura Carter

Look At What We Had

The world,
A vast, wondrous place,
Once.
Not now.
Now all has turned to dust -
Cities have crumbled,
Oceans are dry,
Mountains have fallen,
Why?
Because man thought he was God.
He played with fire, and didn't burn,
So he thought he was better than his creator.
Who could better their creator?
Man scorned his planet, his gift,
He turned his back on his god,
He invented his destruction,
By his own hands, man was destroyed.
The heavens fell,
Angels lost their wings,
And Hell rose to earth.
Satan and his fires burned all that was not already forfeit,
And when the fire eventually ate itself,
Only this was left.
The Gods - lost
Mother Earth - barren
The human race committed mass suicide.

The world -
It's a wonderful place.

Marie Ryan

My Dreaded Future

The world that's coming not too late
I'm sure it won't be nature's mate
Robots in charge I just know
Pollution makes no more snow.

Most animals dead in the wood
People will be on GM food
Oil slicks cover the ocean
We'll be left without a solution.

All the playground games we play
Computers will take away
Many cities made in space
A trip to the moon will be the case.

Science and technology will flourish
Place for mankind will soon vanish
All the mess will give us flu
I dread it and I bet you do.

Even though we wish and pray
It'll be our fault anyway
But we will try and help our earth
Give the future a secure birth.

Narthana Ilenkovan

PERFECT WORLD

My perfect world would be -
Beautiful,
As beautiful as could be -
No more fighting
No more guns,
No more killing
No more slums,
No more poverty
And no more pollution.

I'd like all cars to vanish,
Which are choking up the land.
I'd like all animals
To be set free -
And I'd like them all to know me -
For what I want for them.
I really want this world to be,
Perfect,
As perfect as could be!

Sara Hutchby (11)

WILDLIFE!

I think there should be more wild animals in the wild,
To make the wildlife more wilder.
I also think that we should have wildlife in Britain,
Because you want to travel to Africa all the time to see the wild,
So if you have it in Britain,
It is nearer and you'll be able to feed it or maybe see it every day,
I think the baby tigers are cute because they are only young and little,
But as they grow older, bigger and wilder
I don't like them because they are scary and they can eat you up.
I also like koalas because they are nice,
And they climb up trees all day,
I think there should be more trees so the koalas
Can have their own trees each instead of fighting all the time.
That is what I like about wildlife.

Emma Sloan (12)

WHAT IS THE PURPOSE OF LIFE?

What is the purpose of life?
Why were we put here
On this blue and green sphere
Called Earth?

Why did God make us?
There must have been a reason
For choosing man as part of
His masterplan.

Did God want us to be his toys?
Little dolls that would share and give
And could happily live
In his world.

Then what happened to his perfect plan?
Were his dolls supposed to kill and hate
And leave the world in such a state
As it is now?

Were we put here to start famine and wars?
To destroy the lives of each other?
He did not make guns and bombs and set
Brother against brother.

Each of us was put here for a reason.
God doesn't make mistakes.
He's given us one chance on Earth to show we can
Make a difference.

Through our lives we can share happiness and love
And change the wrong to right.
But first we must forget one line -
'I, Me and Mine'.

Joanne Kerr (14)

WORLD IN THE FUTURE

In the future I see:

People will be able to go on holiday in space,
And also will go time travelling.
In hospitals either scientists or doctors
will find a cure for cancer.
Virtual reality might become everyday life.
Most people might do genetic engineering.
We better watch out because not a single
person knows what lays around the corner
It could be a meteorite.

Simone Tallis

Racism

R ussian
A frican
C hinese
I ndian
S panish
M aybe in the future people will
    realise we are all the same.

Stella Hambly (12)

BAN THE GIRLS

Girls, girls, I don't understand them,
For the boys' sake,
Why don't they ban them?

They all like Nick from the Backstreet Boys,
With his cheesy smile, and his nail file.
They all like Ronan from Boyzone,
He never leaves home without a hair comb.

Girls, girls I don't understand them,
For the boys' sake,
Why don't they ban them?

They concentrate on being as thin as a stick,
And their brain is as thick as a brick.
They never confess, that they think they're the best,
And they never admit, that their hair is a mess.

Girls, girls, I don't understand them,
For the boys' sake,
Why don't they ban them?

They all like Lee from 911
Everything he sings is a disaster song.
They're so picky, they don't play sports in the rain,
All I say is 'No pain no game!'

Girls, girls I don't understand them,
For the boys' sake,
Why don't they ban them?

Jordan Fothergill (11)

BOYS ARE USELESS

Look at that boy
He's a smart toy.
He can't even kick
He's like a stick,
My brother cries
When he lies.
Boys think they're the best
When they pass their test,
Boys think they're old
When their hair is bold.
Boys are cute
They're like a flute,
And some are OK
And some obey.

Katie Vickery (11)

BOYS! BOYS! BOYS!

Boys are funny, football mad.
'Go on Man U make me glad'
Tom said that yesterday, after he came
out to play,
John's pathetic,
He thinks he's cool.
But he's not, he's just a fool.
Tim is stupid,
He's a pain.
That's why we call him Mr Complain.
Joey he's OK a bit
Only because he's kind and fit.

Mikki Tozer (10)

Mad Ladz!

Boys in our school are like any other lad
They moan and groan, and their brain is as small as a pea.
Boys in our school think they're cool and big but they're just fools.
Most of them are football crazy and they're definitely not lazy.
They're very sporty and cute (some of them).
They shout in class
But they make you laugh.
Some can be good friends.

Jenna Linley (10)

TOTAL FOOLS

Boys think they're cool . . .
But, really they're fools
They spit *yuk!*
And most of them can't cook!
They shout real loud *(pass the ball)*
Like a very big crowd
Boys think they're the best
But if we put them to the test
They'll find out girls are the best
And when they're playing football and trying to
Score a goal well have you seen them?
They hit the pole!
All they do is sit around and moan but sometimes,
Girls have a groan
Some try and do their best . . .
But they're like the rest!
So in years to come they might be number one . . .
But don't count on it!

Louise Denham (10)

THE GIRL IN OUR SCHOOL

There's a girl in our school,
She thinks she's really cool.
She answers all questions even when
She hasn't got a clue.
Sometimes she can be kind,
Sometimes she can be cruel.
But all in all girls still think they rule.

Leigh Warsop (10)

WHY DO WE NEED 'EM?

Boyz,
They don't share because they're sad,
Did I mention they're mad?
They think they're cool,
When they break a school rule.
But if you ask me they're
Silly fools

Except for the Backstreet Boys of course,
Because they're so *saucy!*

Jodie Harper (10)

THE BRAINBOX

There's a brainbox in my school,
Who thinks he's really cool.
He calls some of us babe
And some of us sexy legs.
He has been out with all us girls in one year.
Then one day he went to Miss Boydell
'Miss I've been out with every girl in this boring school
So will you go out with me?'
Now Miss was as red as a tomato.
But I think he is cute with
His blond hair and blue eyes. Really.

Nichola Broughton (11)

THE BOY OF HER DREAMS

He came towards her,
his big blue eyes sparkling,
his black hair glinting in the afternoon sun.
His sparkling eyes fastened on hers,
warmth, love and happiness,
seemed to glow in his eyes.

She stood breathlessly on the sand,
as she waited for him.
When he reached her,
he held out his strong hands to her,
and just as she was about to take them,
he seemed to vanish into the air.

She woke up in a cold sweat,
never again did she have this dream,
but his sparkling blue eyes and
his glinting black hair
was never, ever forgotten.

Denise Clarken

MY BROTHER

My brother is a pain,
He is so insane.
He moans and groans
And screams all day,
So in the end he makes me say,
'Now that's it you've done it now,
You've made Mum get irritable bowel.'
'Charging her around all day
You wait, one day she'll make you pay.'

Laura Mason

THE PAINS!

Boys think they are cool
They think they rule the school,
They are always saying they're bad
But they are sad,
They have the playground
With the boring football,
When they are told to do something
They never do it,
I hate boys!
They never do work in school
Boys are just cruel.
They think they're the teacher,
I think they try and tell us what to do.
But they are just pains!

Faye Tutin (11)

BOYS ARE NOT STRONG

Boys just think about football,
but some are OK
They get carried away with fighting,
but some are OK
They think they are better than us girls,
but they're not.
Some kick and some hit,
but some are OK
They think they are strong
but they are wrong.

Vikki Lee (11)

FIDDLING GIRLS

Girls, girls, girls, always fiddling with clips and curls.
They're either filing their nails,
Or making up tales.
They're always using their lipstick
Couldn't they just use a chapstick.
Have you noticed they're always whispering?
You never know what they're saying,
You feel like a fly who is blistering!

Patrick Law (10)

JEALOUS GIRLS!

Girls are always arguing
because they're jealous,
they're so, so, so bossy, it's unbelievable!

I don't play with girls,
They think they're pretty by wearing make-up
And they've sometimes got their hair in pearls.
I don't like girls at all,
Because they drive me up the wall!

Lee Barnes (10)

BLOOMIN' BOYS

Boys think they're the best
Well, let's put them to the test . . .
Boys think they're cool,
But, really, they're fools.
They can't score a goal,
They hit the bloomin' pole.
Boys smell, and tell.
They like to think they're the brains,
But, really, they're just a bunch of pains.
They roll around in the muck,
And they definitely can't cook!
Boys show off,
And pretend to boff.
The teachers are always shouting at boys,
Because they're always bringing toys.
They don't appreciate school,
They just sit there thinking they're cool.
They throw nasty fits
I think they're just big gits.
Boys don't bath or wash
And they're *definitely* not posh!
They don't give a toss,
And they love playing with moss!
They think they rule,
Everyone at school.
Snip, snap, snout,
This tale's told out!

Gemma Campbell (11)

BOYS!

Boys are crazy about footie,
boys are crazy about food.
They sleep, spit and tell rude jokes
- it's terrible.
They say we mess with our looks
but you should see 'em.
They look like hedgehogs!
Girls are totally different,
We're cool!
I don't understand boys.
Well, you can't live with 'em,
can live without 'em!

Kimberley Phoenix (11)

MAD, BAD BOYZ

'Boyz! Mad, bad boyz!' all us girls say
'Should go away and not come back another day!
All of us (well it's clear to se) we're clever
They're thick, thick as leather.
What we hate though is, for footie, some of us girls being requested
Yet others are being badgered and pestered
So hear us out. *Quit it!* It's *not* funny!
What *is* funny though is him and his mates
Trying to be cool on their rollerblades or skates
they try (with their so-called remarkable skill) to bowl us over
But just end up knocking us over instead.
Oh, by the way, who says they've got remarkable skill?
Them of course! Big headed, arrogant babies who think they're cuties,
Wearing their tiny little booties!
In class you should see them 'Cor blimey!'
They rant and rave like a big savage army!
One thing is certainly for sure
They're rude, uncaring, contemptuous and so-o-o-o immature.
They can't resist taking little sips
Of their fathers' beers or lagers
Along with a hamburger and chips
We tell them the truth that they're just big twits
Because they won't leave us alone telling us they fancy us to bits!
You say you can't understand us
Well we can't (as you've just found out) understand you!
Boyz! Mad, bad boyz!' all us girls say
'Should go away and not come back another day!'

Lyndsey Staples (11)

BOYS ARE SO ANNOYING

Boys are so annoying,
but girls are simply grand.
Boys just watch the telly,
whilst girls lend a hand.

Girls they wear nice pink dresses,
with frilly bows in their hair.
While boys wear jeans and a T-shirt,
if they look scruffy they just don't care.

Boys play a game called football,
or romp in the mud all day.
Whilst girls with friends sit and chat,
They're so much quieter in their play.

Well as you can see boys are a nuisance,
they are disgusting, dirty and mean.
While girls are so much nicer,
they are pretty, polite and clean.

Chantel Lees (12)

GIRLS ON BOYS

Boys are these
crawly things
which suddenly
appear, pop out of nowhere and
seem to disappear

Some people say it's their
hormones but I seem to wonder
because as they are screaming
and shouting they sound like
roaring thunder.

Michelle Hall (12)

GIRL POWER

My sister is nice, sweet and spice
Always wise with bright eyes
When I'm bad she gets mad
Lends a hand when I'm sad.

Gentle in mind, true and kind
Nicest person one can find
Helpful, friendly and polite
Having her around is a delight.

Spends her time with a book
She has a very nice look
Talks about the girl power
A great singer in the shower.

I have told you quite a lot
About a sister I have got
I tried to tell the very best
But nothing real . . . to be honest!

Aruthiran Ilenkovan

A THOUGHTFUL DESCRIPTION

He was standing there again today.
When he looked at me, I looked away.

He was warring his blue denim jacket
With holes in his front pocket.

He got on the No 47 bus:
And I really wished that, I was.

Whenever I'm standing at the bus stop,
I think of him, and his smile.

I saw him today with a girl in my class,
He held her hand, and walked away fast.

I cried for days after that
Because the boy I liked would never be mine.

Amanda Shields (13)

WEIRD GIRLS

The girls in our school,
Hang around and pretend to be cool.
They talk about the film last night,
Where Arnold Schwarzenegger won a fight.
They adore
Batty, Seaman and Solskjaer.
They're so immature and silly,
They scream and shout when they meet popstar Billie.
Us lads are getting quite brassed off,
Because, on us, they always seem to cough.

Ashley Butler (11)

BOYS BOYS BOYS

Some boys are so nice
Some boys are kind
Some boys are annoying but
I don't really mind.

Some boys share and
Some boys care.

Some boys rap and
Some boys tap.

Karla Barclay (11)

SILLY GIRLS

Girls,
Think they rule but they drool
They think they look cool.
Girls
Make themselves look glamorous
But! They always make a bodge,
They wear high heels but they
Always
Fall over.

Lewis Aaron James (11)

DIRTY PAT

I know a boy called Patrick
everybody calls him Pat
he's dirty and annoying
he's smelly and rather fat.

First of all Pat's hair was blond
but now it's thick with grease
everyone knows he never changes his clothes
as through his trousers you can clearly see his knees.

Kathleen Laura Neilson (10)

GIRLS ON BOYS

Boys, boys, boys,
they keep the world going round,
girls need them to live,
girls need them to love.

What would us girls do
with no boys in the world,
no one to love,
no one to marry,
no one to introduce to our mummy.

Boys listen,
boys understand.
Boys are always there
to lend a hand.
Boys, boys, boys.

Sarah Loxton (13)

SOME BOYS

Some boys are great!
They make you laugh,
And comfort you when you're in a state.
Some buy you a meal,
Or take you out,
And show you what living's all about!
They make you feel good about yourself,
And that you're not second best.

Others can hurt,
They be mean and treat you like dirt.
They sometimes take advantage,
Or pretend you're not there.
They can frustrate you,
And make you feel worthless.
(When this happens you thank God for chocolate,
Video and girl mates.)

Boys do weird things when asking you out,
Some are mean, pull your hair, scream and shout,
Then ask you out.
Some are shy and daren't ask you things,
Especially when you're dying to be asked.
But the remaining few are nice,
And just ask you straight.
It's these boys that are great!

Samantha Wilton

BOYS ON GIRLS!

I think boys act hard;
But when you think of it,
They are very mard.
Boys probably
think we girls
are ugly
in the
looks.

But we are good at reading
books. We think boys are
good at football.
Boys think we
are bad,
that gets
us really
mad!

Carla Stanway (10)

BROTHERS

B oys are naughty,
   They are bad,
O gre faces when they are mad.
   Pathetic faces when they are sad!
Y ucky noises my brothers make,
   They always have a frown on their face.
S o as you can see,
   Brothers do not please me!

B oys are noisy,
   They make lots of sound,
O h! They always seem to be around!
   They like to leap, jump and bound.
Y es! They like to stuff themselves with cake.
   I did teach them to tie a lace
S orry to say
   I do really love them!

Ashleigh Rouse (10)

JUST A MEMORY

Such a crying shame
I wish it wasn't so
I hope she never suffered
I really loved her so

But now she has been taken
There's no return you see
Our beautiful Diana
Just a memory.

Alan Green

FULL HOUSE

There was a lady in Crewe,
Who, had many children,
Well more than a few,
With such wedded bliss,
If it continued like this, with yet another due,
Anyone could see,
The future would be as the old woman - who lived in a shoe!

Benny Howell

TITANIC

On a cold morning on April 15, 1912, Titanic sunk
In the early hours of the morning.
It was a big gash, 300ft long, that was made by an iceberg
Into the Titanic, but in actual fact it was a small visible slit.
Mr Andrews said it would stay afloat on the first four compartments
But five of them are filled.
People screaming, jumping off into the icy waters.
Rich women and children in the lifeboats first.
All the poor people drowning as Titanic goes down head first.
Titanic is half and half, the stern is up in the air
As the bow goes further in. As she splits the ship has broken.
The stern splashes and pushes the lifeboats further away.
As the stern rises one more time it sinks slowly
But the ship is still in one piece.
Then she is halved in two.
The bow goes down, slow rocking back and forth
As it reaches a sudden stop the mud is ploughed up.
The stern is half a metre away from the bow
And parts of the ship lie in the middle.
And this is called Titanic Graveyard.

Daniel Reid (13)

SUBMISSIONS INVITED
SOMETHING FOR EVERYONE

POETRY NOW '99 - Any subject,
any style, any time.

WOMENSWORDS '99 - Strictly women,
have your say the female way!

STRONGWORDS '99 - Warning!
Age restriction, must be between 16-24,
opinionated and have strong views.
(Not for the faint-hearted)

All poems no longer than 30 lines.
Always welcome! No fee!
Cash Prizes to be won!

Mark your envelope (eg *Poetry Now*) **'99**
Send to:
Forward Press Ltd
Remus House, Coltsfoot Drive,
Woodston,
Peterborough, PE2 9JX

OVER £10,000 POETRY PRIZES
TO BE WON!

Judging will take place in October 1999